THE FAMILY CHINA

THE FAMILY CHINA

Ann Shin

BRICK BOOKS

Library and Archives Canada Cataloguing in Publication

Shin, Ann
    The family china / Ann Shin.

Poems.
ISBN 978-1-926829-80-7

    I. Title.

PS8587.H4786F34 2013 .   C811'.6   C2013-900989-2

Second Printing - October 2013

We acknowledge the Canada Council for the Arts, the Government of Canada through the Canada Book Fund, and the Ontario Arts Council for their support of our publishing program.

 Canada Council for the Arts   Conseil des Arts du Canada    Government of Canada   Gouvernement du Canada

The author and cover photos were taken by Sandy Nicholson.

This book is set in Minion Pro, designed by Robert Slimbach and released in 1990 by Adobe Systems.

Design and layout by Cheryl Dipede.
Printed and bound by Sunville Printco Inc.

Brick Books
431 Boler Road, Box 20081
London, Ontario N6K 4G6
www.brickbooks.ca

To my family

CONTENTS

FORGOTTEN FIELDS	1
FACTORIES OF DISCONTENT	17
SPEED OF NOW	37
LOVESHORN	49
WE ARE WHAT WILL BECOME OF US	61
ACKNOWLEDGEMENTS	73
BIOGRAPHICAL NOTE	77

FORGOTTEN FIELDS

Pressing sponges to the wall as water dripped from elbows,
they gift-wrapped the insides of a farmhouse gone to bush.
We weren't allowed in 'til moving day, then
we ran through the rooms like it was Christmas.

A plastic-wrapped window bed, a warm spot by the wood stove.
We claimed corners of the house with our dolls, our bodies
knitting in with this place that so wanted kids.
Trees sprouted apples, cherries dropped from heavy boughs.

The farmhouse mellowed, ripened, held secrets so long
infinity bloomed as wind lifted the curtains,
leaves dusted shadows across his face
as fleeting as day, inchoate like the night.
My brother fell asleep with his heel banging the wall.

Now wallpaper peels like petals drying on the stem.
You can fit half a kid between the dark walls,
the other half floats somewhere over the fields
where dew dots long grass stalks and cows rub against
gate posts. Clean nicks. Chapped lips. Wet hair.

Fingers flutter over the barbed-wire fence
where he fell. Black stitches on cold, white skin.
Through the still water of a round glass vase
the yard primps perennials in pink and yellow –
refulgent, they live again, as they do each spring.

A cow lumbers past, rubs the fence post again.
A moth dusts my fingers and is gone. The earth's mantle
folds, forming a skin over my brother's body
and I am wedged between wooden slats, not breathing.

dew : summer nights I ran through cul-de-sacs like a dog on the loose, past houses stretched out on ample haunches, each black-tarred driveway another notch in a ruler that ended in a grassy field where I stopped for breath beneath the well of the midnight sky, PJ bottoms wet with dew

My mother washed the walls of that house
with the assurance of those who see order in chaos,
doors flung wide to butterflies trussing their beds outside
among weeds, tumbled hay bales, twisted apple trees.
I never caught a butterfly all the summers we lived there
never tried enough, afraid of crushed wings releasing
orange-yellow dust into the night breeze.
My mother's breath at my ear freed me into sleep
while luscious fields edging up to my window
swished their long grasses onto my carpet.
Slipping headlong I slept like a riverbank,
waves lapping against my velvet clay chest.
Few words were spoken, even fewer remembered
for I'm still half submerged.

chaos: after her accident the house fell into decline, fruit flies like blackheads stippled rotting pears, packs of Bic pens sat atop the TV next to rolled-up tube socks, crinkled newspaper caught in the spokes of my mother's wheelchair as she pushed herself from room to room

The practiced hand of progress
did its surgery on our village,
its skin razed concrete-smooth,
raspberry thickets, knotted roots and stones
peeled back like thick handfuls of scalp.
The mind startles.

A crop of beige houses sprouts up erect,
the celebrated seeds of eugenic success,
while weathered barns and wooden fences crumple under.
The seams of a yellowed map – its *terra incognita*
glimmers in the dusk of our awareness.

Now no location is unknown
and places we secretly inhaled
like the scent of our bed pillows
are lost in the static of an electric night;
this is the sound of our proliferation
as we pillage ourselves in darkness,
scattered points of light.

handfuls: when *halmunee* made miso, she pushed her hands into the fermented soy, rubbing handfuls together to test their softness *some people count days but the only way to know is by feel*

Meticulously ravenous,
the plane erases all that I call my own.
Forceps pull weight through customs,
a body – not mine but an occupancy en route –
pulls the seat up, remembers roaming
the fields like a dog off the leash and
huddling to pee under a giant hemlock
as the carpool mom drove by, calling, calling.

We were farm kids going nowhere.
We have everywhere now
and it has us.

fields: runt of five brothers, dad worked the cold rice fields, the soles of his feet puckered white   at lunch they passed around a wool jacket to keep warm, shared a bowl of barley and anchovies

The city's intersections dilate in the slick night.
We course the dark streets in our fathers' cars
along roads too narrow to contain our desire.
Bass rhythms reverberate through double-brick walls.
Overshooting our mark we topple hotdog carts
on a taxi ride through midnight's suburbs,
our parents' dreams a safe haven beside fields
of transformers buzzing with febrile intensity.
Children in their nightgowns stand waiting to sing,
as the song skips a generation.

Roll me down the length of your long, black driveway.
Let's steal back what's ours from closed-mouth houses
where lights are left on, mail delivered, lawns mowed,
while we're out on the hunt in dew-wet fields
hungry to find and twist open the seed
of our own promise. We're not lost,
we've just been looking away.

safe: your *yiayia* unlocked her walnut safebox and handed you her gold necklace with its simple, heavy links   *give to her,* she said   your tanned hands fumbled as you held it round my neck, clasping me into the loop

Palms ascending to span
the two shores within us,
my family left their country, and I them,
for this side of the ocean.
A continent rolls over,
nudging us westward

        as a rising tide
fills and erases our tracks.
Ancient ravines choked with asphalt,
a sky bristling with office buildings –
the emerging face is a geometry
mapped with the crisp clarity
of intersections.

As dreams, in desperate fluids,
find sluicepoints in gutter gateways,
we appear and disappear
like reflections in a puddle,
echoed in this landscape
but not of it.

fill: *yiayia* admonished you to fill your plate, and so you returned, slim whip of a man carrying an overladen dish   my folks taught me to clear my plate, but not to eat my fill   this I am still learning

They moved to the country
leaving me their house,
an undead corpse I must rob
with rubber gloves, garbage bags.

On the walls are blank outlines,
parentheses where once stood
bookcases, sofa sets. Boxes labelled
'photos' and 'kitchen miscellaneous' gone.

The intricate bric-a-brac
that shaped my world, disassembled –
whatever key they took with them
locked up the meaning of things.

A tracing of lost hair, skin,
a scattering of nail clippings,
in a house of well-worn paths
now abandoned, like assumptions
from a bygone era.

As for me, I wish to leave
subtle, indelible marks.
I will enter and exit your heart
like a breeze flowing through a room,
transforming the very air.

country: dad brought mom to Canada during the Trudeau years, when the bachelor Prime Minister twirled the country onto the world stage like a shy girl in a starched prom dress *we make the future here,* dad said, and started the chase

The rule-maker drops her gavel
so I busy myself good and proper
before the kids come home sensing
something wrong, the way they do, their
eyes larger than their souls, silent cavities,
ruined churches. Their open hands, like
silky hymn books in the rain, are missing pages.
Standing in their nightgowns they wait for the
first sonorous notes. Where is the organist?

One day I hope to stand with them in their silent pews
so they may trust that I, their living spokesperson,
remember the tune.

I thought I loved, then held my breath,
exhaled: yes you yes me, we exist
and vanish in a turnkey the
washing machine lets loose
secrets wrapped in the gyre
of folding and refolding you, love
stake the place where we'll build our life,
clothe it with bricks, rituals weightier
than desire or habitual kisses.

Drive me to the outskirts with the gas close to empty,
I'll run in the dark until I'm breathless, sweaty,
and find my way home by the light of our porch.

outskirts: your *pappous* built a home for him and *yiayia* no electricity, a dirt road, two dozen head of mountain goats and an uncontested piece of land

A hush on the phone, a dropped moment
and you are all underbrush, ferns,
delicate plants curling from sun.
I press on, my words a shadow-puppetry
of light falling to the damp earth with its
fungal undergrowth of silent unfurlings:
between every 'no' is a curtailed 'yes'
latticing its spores beneath the forest floor
to poke through rotting leaves; in the furrowed
bark of a tree, under mossy rocks bloom
soft white gills of attention.

Oh this is what it is to say yes in a hundred places,
tiny hands pushing out from in,
this is love working its surgery on me,
all my hearts opening and closing
their valves as I breathe.

sun: we wrapped the tablecloth around us, the one *yiayia* had embroidered, as rain fell on our picnic, turning into hail the size of gumballs, the sky pelting us with sudden sun

Hunched on a clump of island, our chests heaving,
waves whipping, we watch the light fall,
only twenty minutes from shore, from the call
of bedtime stories, slammed drawers
and dinners sitting cold on the stove. The storm
hasn't reached home – will never arrive there.

Out here, we stand cold and simple in our skin,
stripped and compassless, we are but
water, wind, and the will to get home.
We do what we are called to,
our tired arms pinwheeling
like gulls at sea, or like
hearing aids at the opera,
pacemakers during sex –
that is to say, we are ill-equipped

to re-trim the jib our listing sailboat
whose mast jitters like a frantic seismograph
charting turmoil as we roll in again
toward harbour.

slammed: when I moved out of my parents home unmarried, un-engaged, un-anything, my father slammed the door and locked it, then opened it and ran full tilt, trying to catch me

A pillowed hill for my daughter's head
and a farm under each leg,
so she may sup nightly on dreams of
fields in Quebec whose clean lines
are a well-practiced penmanship.
Sweat-blonde hay slicked back for
picture day. A fresh coat of red paint.
Fields of peaches-and-cream corn.

Something to be said for
doing the same ol' thing well,
take Le Ciel de Charlevoix
or rounds of Le Baluchon –
the taint of human hands, the
musty earth and its chewed cud,
are brought together in the
alchemy of a single bite;
we are hauled by our senses
back to a place of belonging.

This world mapped in earthy tones
is what I would give to my daughter,
a sensorial GPS of the soul
with an astrolabe sighting
the moon and planets;
a flock of geese aligning into a V,
pointing to where the cows are happy,
cheese is rich, and there's no rust in the buckets.

belonging: in my father's closet are suitcases tightly packed with striped suits from the 70s, orange ties to match, a Korean *hambok* from the 50s, a 1971 Toronto bus schedule, yellowed pages from a journal titled *Five-Year Plan*

It lay in the bog among velvet-brown leaves,
one wing flung out as if, groping for the sky,
it missed.

Half-drowned
among brambled branches veiled
by sky submerged in water.

Spindly feet curled
like the blackened tines of a fork
lost in the rubble of a burnt house.

Bent beams
and a skewed horizon,
a tangle of thoughts in free fall.

All this
pathos and pastoral imagery ain't
getting me nowhere.

house: swallows fly in and out through your grandparents' first home, fire having blackened the stone walls, ravaged the thatched roof, leaving empty rooms flayed open to the sky

FACTORIES OF DISCONTENT

A miscellany of complaints trellises our garden.
Despite the wicker mess the concrete stands its ground.
We climb pastwise up from the foundation
through subfloors criss-crossed with hanging lights,
half-walls open onto a skewed horizon.
We shout at one another from different floors.
No stairs to span the distance. Bent beams,
uncoupled like staves of dropped notes,
echo into darkness a collapsing tune.

If every argument were the retraction of love
our relationship would be drawn in zigzag lines,
the pen scratching, grinding through to receptive wood.
You plant your broad foot and extend your hand–

                              Pull me up love,
let's get ourselves out of this fix.

tune: *what's that you're whistling?* was the line you used *I don't know,* I shrugged   you grinned, *I do*

The many-fingered avalanche of desire
slides down the mirrors of our house,
collecting in pools to seep into floorboards.
It finds its lowest point; we amass there
suppurating in silence.

Apathy is a scar long since closed over.
Board it up as the kids trample in
with brilliant resilience.
A pink cactus flower blossoms
on the Christmas window ledge;
the tenacity of a house plant
heeding anterior seasons.
We toss aside the wrappings
and shoo the kids to bed.

tuck: mom kept her own stashes, *halmunee's* letters in the cabinet, a folded poem in the hollow beneath the sewing machine needle foot, pieces of cut fabric tucked away for a dress never completed

A drawer opens and closes,
and the whole shebang shines
with the malevolence of a
household object held wrong,

but when it's tendered right
in the palm of our hands,
how smoothly it all tucks in.
A child climbs into bed,
pulls the duvet to her chin
as hot water splashes
into a dirty kitchen sink.

Piece by piece we pick apart the orange
as if sunshine were ours to kill and eat.
I undial the leaves to slow things down.
You are a long-distance call telling me
everything is alright, but the hours
have unlimbed themselves,
grown vague and weary,
ending up in pre-dawn Emergency.

I am a crushed foot, a heart attack,
two hands crashing down on
an electric piano with no speakers;
I am an organist in a dark house
where every toothbrush, every sock,
every dinner plate on the counter is
a testament to other, unbuilt developments;
I am a briefcase filled with glossy brochures,
the pith of every great endeavour pulled to pieces,
and nothing to show for it. Juice runs down my arms.

emergency: they came, flashing red lights in the dark night, and strapped in mom's arms and legs, propping her head slowly, carefully   there was a pool of blood in the barn basement where she fell   I don't know who cleaned up

Desire, the ewe that mothers our expectations,
pulls us slapdaggling into the future, seeking
comfortably round-syllabled assertions that yes,
things are destined, there is natural progression
and love, like prejudice, is a gut instinct.

But desire's salvo of shots misses
its mark, like semen sprayed wrong;
we lie spent, dissatisfied
as the hour closes its mind.
In a sundown shower your fingers
find the pulse of retribution.

Gathering at the dinner table
we shuffle pieces of cutlery,
building factories of our discontent.

yes: *ready?* dad asked as I stood by the door with thread wrapped around my tooth   I nodded, sensing this was one of those questions to which one can only respond yes

A rubber glove tugged off
reveals a hand and the shape
of what it is to be contained.

How a stranger becomes a love,
and love becomes familiar,
the familiar hated.

The form holds:
estrangement
of me through you.

estrangement:
after her accident
my toes went
numb, then my
feet, my face, my
lips   I walked
to school in the
morning, checking
the redness of my
chapped hands to
tell if I was cold

Yes the conversation
was good wasn't good –
minor strokes erupt at brunch
leaving partial paralysis
in the attempt to express
the cloven heart.

We are ruminants regurgitating
habitual internal gestures.
Between my side and yours
are miles of antlers
and nimble conversation.
Lapping it up so good, we are
good-faced and busy
despite minor incontinences,
doing fine thank you, the bill
makes sense if not us.

forks: your *thia* and *yiayia* sorted through the burnt rubble rescuing blackened spoons, forks with curled tines   they polished and bundled them into 5 handkerchiefs, one for each grandchild

If arms were wishbones I'd toss off
a dozen embraces for you and me
and the rest of us stubbornly unloved.
Let the knives and forks have it out
as we find our feet again, somewhere
among the broken china.

A lineage of ancestors
inhabits the universe of our minds:
constellations, etching fence lines against
the dark field, spell things like *I love you
for what you represent*, meaning
those stories we're meant to live
but never live up to: our country,
our kids, our undivorced heartaches,
ourselves.

We decided we wanted this but
lost the sense of it, a scatter-shot
of bullet point to-do lists
waking the silver-haired denizens
who shamble into the fields, telling us
You've got it all wrong.

It's getting late. The mall parking lot
is dotted with doors closing and
I'm pushing my cart, still looking.
Could love please be placed
in aisle 3 somewhere prominent,
I've lost my passport to that easier country.

mall: my first
cigarette, my first
makeover, my first
real leather purse, my
first teetering steps in
high heels   I roamed
through Cloverdale
Mall anxious
to acquire
all the trappings

Shopping mall parking lots dotted with doors
closing, this is the time of our parting.
A melody hummed in the head, this country
peopled with stop signs and trees whose
autumn leaves still fixed on dark branches
undrop in sunlit snow.

You and I,
we've had legions of winter
and technically speaking
the transmission is crisp.
I am
a blank shot
waiting to be fired.

transmission: *it transmits okay, your dad pointed to his ear, but hearing aids only amplify what the ear hears and if the ear can't hear, well...*

The contract lies between us, a relic from our early days,
a positioning paper like a UN peace proposal
where participant countries keep changing boundaries,
claiming new territory, then resort to mortar fire.

Or like a quote for renovating a house
with lots of character but bad insulation:
we knew, though we're just discovering
the deeper structural issues.

Winters come, we layer ourselves
in second and third skins. We huddle,
getting our sea legs as the floor slants,
the house settles.

> **settle**: dad called to
> talk about money, fights
> between brothers,
> fights with mom's family,
> money spent to raise
> us kids, about *money
> doesn't grow on trees,
> and even if I don't have
> money, who needs your
> money anyway?* stop
> yelling, I said,
> *no one's arguing with you*
> he didn't seem to hear
> so I set the receiver
> down on a chair,
> and waited

If all we ever were thrust through
the pillows over our mouths,
would we rest our heads, accept
that our dreams have incubated for too long?

The papers report a misuse of funds
stemming from skewed fundamentals.
In frantic recalculation we hit on
a windfall of consciousness:
time to cut losses.

Duty pulls us back from the edge
and talks us through to the other side.
Duty is the Tupperware dish
that saves the steak we barely tasted
for tomorrow, there is always tomorrow
in this endlessly remodelled town.
Round the corner, up the alley
following the leeside of the mountain,
you may not find it but keep going
the route will lead you on.

steak: tough, thick, the meat was different from the *bulgoki* mom always made   dad took a kitchen knife to it, saying, *this is what the Rockefellers eat*

Slamming the fridge door an egg
slips from my fingers –
             cracks
        and splats
into a gelatinous puddle.

Unlike chipped cups or fraying sweaters,
fermenting fruit and worn hinges
or any manner of household object,
including ourselves –
you drop an egg
and it's game over,
a sphere of potentiality
broken.

I survey the mess at my feet
and bend down with a rag
to wipe it up.

A keening
rises to the skin,
weeps.

fermenting:
custodians of the art
of fermenting, your
yiayia hung balls of
cheese curd from a
clothesline in Cyprus
my *halmunee* laid
out bricks of miso
on a verandah in
Vancouver   they
knew food, when to
harvest, when to let
things break down
and ferment

A tinderbox,
the light in your eyes
wants kindling,
the breaking of furniture legs,
unstuffing of upholstery.

Let's have it out, shall we?
Hurl everything through windows
fracturing surfaces
we'd grown to believe solid

and get scraped down
to the breastbone,
a searing clean.

A limpid moment
within shape-changing rooms
where the wind blows softly
like water in a fish's gills.

Those living barbs embedded themselves deep
when you were a kid, grafting into skin,
slipping upstream to your heart muscle.

They lie dormant until you're
pierced again by that hive of pain,
vomiting wasps. Old familiar thing.
Is it me or is it you? We do
what couples often do.

I go out and nurse a coffee,
watch the cream form a skin
then gulp the whole thing down.

vomit: it came like a sudden orgasm, an upswelling in my chest and clean jerk into my aunt's rosebushes in the dead of night my first drink sick I wiped my mouth clean, joyous release I got rid of it, got rid of all of it

A year of transitions, breakups, volcanoes –
I distrust the land, all feelings,
am millennial in my mistakes.

The earth falls away and my hands
hold an idea beneath my feet,
underpinning a path of aspirations
as a continent knuckles under, twisting
with ever-more-inward contusions.

Our frontiers are internal now,
border crossings subject to new regulations.
Hermeneutic guards let slip the odd communication –
a bottle in the ocean, a note left under a stone,
an email washing up on the shore of that distant
sunlit continent.

hands: your father greets me with his big hands fanned out, deep grooves, orange calluses at the base of each finger   when he hugs me I am solid, entitled to my place on earth

Tyranny is easier to face than beneficence –
at least you know what you're dealing with.
With this crabwise logic we find each other's
weaknesses, poke our fingers and watch the bruises
bloom full terror. Economic sanctions are levied
but the regime digs in. Nothing comes in/goes out.
Reports show returns are lower than expected
and casualties keep creeping up, while downstairs
in the basement the boiler keeps boiling.

casualties: *an island divided is a body cleaved in pain,* said *yiayia*, perched on her pine stool, her coffee cradled in her thick palm   *not Turkish*, she corrected me, *Cypriot coffee*

O lo soul
on the horizonmost point
where the last singers
sang their psalms –
the tune lingers
though the words have gone.
Can we welcome
first impulse
and say all else
is the time-lapsed
collapse
of age and awareness?
Cast a stone
to skip numerous
rippling sur-
faces
of an ocean
whose depths
are only known
by stones landing
where
the gaze can't go?
Darkness
is not a distance
but a sounding.

Feel the reverberations
reach your distant shores.
Lay your head back, love,
let's compare horizons.

SPEED OF NOW

A running collision of
flesh, sweating metal, noodles
swallowed in airport kiosks,
my cousin's village lies
a stone's throw away
from TV and cell towers,
their footpaths gridded over
with closed-circuit cameras
sending time-lagged images
of what used to be. Your hand
on my heart says you know.
No, nostalgia reeks in this
journey with no parentage;
only velocity defines our most
intricate possession, our selves
in acceleration, reborn
in flights transferred or
hovering over phones,
a whisper in a receiver
is location,
touch –
an escape hatch to other cities
where lost Blackberrys vibrate
with messages unharvested,
fruit returned to the earth
unprofitably; still we
collect ourselves and
paper it up, go public
with initial offerings
of immense growth.

village: on the back of your motorbike drinking *yiayia's* coffee, the grinds so thick and fine there was grit in the back of my teeth for days *help me harvest the olive trees,* she said *I'll get you a cell phone, call me,* you said

PARENTAGE: a list of retirement communities by the phone   my hand hesitates on the receiver   my parents used to be my age they were once all my ages

Push the button of hope:
ideal scenarios play against
eyelids closed for the season,
awaiting new release of the
humanly possible.
Your held breath
stifles impulse,
the way my hands at my sides
when you're in the room
mumble.
        Tell me a tune
mumbled is still a tune.

human: on our second
date you told me you
loved *Bladerunner*
I asked if all androids
long for their mothers

I'll heed your wars less and less,
internal gashes in your scrambled
channels, diseased communiqués
from countries people never go to
for if they go, it remains in their blood.
Peel me, wrap these sores,
I've seen your worst night still
envisioning ceasefire dawns.
Eyes unclosed blood insists
that we, as all life,
go on.
Could I
dwindle
in fits of amnesia?
Hold your hand as we,
weapons dropped,
walk through our
coldest corridors?
Think one step
at a time, rest
a finger on a
piano key?

And surprise a mind
unused to melody.

key: as a student, dad practised piano on a paper keyboard, fingers sliding soundlessly over painted black and white strips   once a week at his teacher's house his fingers pushed down and he heard melody

We attempt procreation
in slim moments of faith
intended for adult use,
but kids pick it up –
the legacy we forgot
to pick up, damaged
ourselves.

  A small trip
and a child's ankle
is a universe of pain.
Oh flesh of mine
continue to swell
with the hope
contained in the jest
that two people
can somehow
make one whole.

legacy: the sound of plates at our wedding when the sambuca shots came out: *to life!* crash! *to life!* *thio* Marcel had the wrong plates, breaking the family china your mom shrieked, your dad grabbed another and smashed it, *to life!*

Close my mouth
stop up holes
that keep spilling,
pray grandma
will always be right.
My new global strategy
requires taking
oblique positions
of risk. To allow
each other's worst
a moment of privacy,
between smiles
of recognition
and internal
combustion,
trust elocution
is the enactment
of instinct
when traditions
no longer hold
our itinerary
of wants and needs.

Ever tightening constrictions
around face, nose, and lips,
your hand opening
a thousand glances,
towering into our
own private
Panopticon,
we are
supplicants wanting
not death but more
life. My country
in contract for
mutual release.

Could you cough it up
in one huge go? Give it
your best now, the minutes
are ticking…

thousand: your
mom glued the
pottery vase
back together,
painstakingly
matching a
thousand chips
and shards   she
placed it back on the
mantle, admired the
jagged new seams

You and I approach
parabolically,
a wishbone curves
into a wish given
then broken,
still wishing.

I'll Fedex my love,
trust it will accrue
vectoral intent
on its journey to you.
Following close is
my body's PS to seal
the mouth of doubt.
The past slants
into the future
upended,
drizzling down
locked windows.
Protected from
yesterday's forecasts

future: *thio's* glazed
pheasant fed us
magnanimously, we
picked it clean down
to its twig-grey bones
found a wishbone

we take wing,
veering off our
migratory paths
as seasons repeat
like television shows,
demanding new casts,
updated wardrobes.

Let's bluesky it, talk plot shifts,
pen entirely different endings,
who says we're locked into anything.

foreknowledge:
go already, you've already left me, your mom wiped her hand across wet brown eyes   we stood in the living room, our packed bags at our feet   *go live your life,* she gave you a fierce hug, then pushed you out the door

Our battlefields camel
the weight of soldiers
whose final imprint in
the soil was their loss,
our gain – the future
portfolioed for kids
who've yet to feel
the ache of earth's
foreknowledge.
The wide-eyed prolapse
of birth paused;
hope
sphincters into
willed intent.
We grope into
that haven
we call
unison.
Together
we are legion –
sound become noise,
wish degenerated
into keyword.
Haven't we read a bunch
of dead men and women?
God save or bookmark
that learned tower,
for posterity
won't answer this yearning.

LOVESHORN

I walk the path to a door that won't open,
        will never fully close.
My longing is a quiet child awake past bedtime,
        nose pressed against wood,
mouth full, nostrils full
        of shovelled dirt

A fury of blood cells pressing against skin,
        I sit tight-lipped
in a car with sealed windows,
        cold air whipping past.
I am a blot of stillness
        volleying through darkness.

All the weeks, months, and years I have lived,
        keep living.
That time is gone,
        he is gone
and the world is not stopping
        for the love of God.

Like a sylph seeking light,
his unturned heart beats arrhythmic
with the excrescence of shrapnel,
not a gun wound but the slow burn
of sickle cells slipping through his
body's tributaries. He smiles blood red
and we cannot staunch the flow.

Old wounds die half-lives, their
poison efflorescing radiological forests
splayed from the brachia of his mind.
Intricately constructed lexical shelves
knuckle under, immaculate walls
collapse, letting all rush in.

Chaos has its own furious design,
his signature forever tangled
with the scribble. Could this
be a way to live? Unintelligible
pandemonium as compelling
as any heart's true moment.

If only I could enter him,
a bead of blood finding its stream
to release in the vena cava
an antidote to make everything
round and whole and safe again.

forest: the tumour grew unnoticed for years, a dark fungus in the forest, until it overtook your *yiayia*'s mind the way a decision can take years to sprout repercussions and you find yourself in the wrong job, the wrong skin, feeling the full-blown effects of the path you have chosen

The sorrow-laden softly fall,
dead skin cells dust the silver sheet.
Steel glimmer of a bedrail
in perpetual medical dusk.
Numb fingers count the
pulse and thank the Lord
for this at least for this.

Pain stops halfway up the IV
where blood meets saline, an alchemy:
life flees your veins, drip by drip
until it's pushed back in.

I kept my ghosts too close at hand.
Dawn slipped in its silver shiv –
bloodless memory, mercurial loss,
my brother is dead, yet still fleeting
and my mother's eyes are the wings of a loon
whose cry heralds a leaving.

Adorn me in the love of the shorn
whose bare feet drag over stones –
no pavement for the lovelorn or
the godless or the fallen

who turn in seismic oceans
to their own feverish undertow.
Darkness fills the mouth foresworn
to not let go or leave forgotten –

a caterwauling car loses its footing
and plunges headlong
                              deeper than asphalt.

shorn: your *yiayia's*
shaking fingers
pointed to the gold
chain around my
neck   she lay
her gleaming head
back on the pillow,
her cold hand
clasping mine, the
strength of her grip
transfixing

Suspended, the follicles rise and fall,
the sheets still, the feet still, eyes still shut.
In coma the seasons pass, shadows lengthen
then vanish, the nails grow, hair shines
with ebullience – the unattended fecundity
of an empty city lot.

Visiting relatives lean against the bed,
breathing evenly without incident.

I watch my mother's face
and feel nothing,
which is when I begin
to feel closest to her.
If this is what she feels,
I want more nothing.

The first blow, the
last official memory.
The tree winters on
without season,
issuing timely signs
of consciousness.
We will moments
to stand in line,
make sense, carry
the official story of a life.

official: brain-dead
they declared her
for 3 long months
dad fought to
keep the plug
plugged in

carry: something
small for 9 months

Breath stilled in the nostrils,
a pulse fights to win the prize.
Flashing numbers in casinos
shout *This is your day!*
Sound the alarm, see if
the ambulance arrives.

The heart trips into
a well of irretrievables.
A bead of blood finds its
quickride into the dark –

shine a flashlight, cover your eyes,
feel with your hands for the opening.

A song sent across the country to my mom
who sleeps as moths flutter from her lips.
I will steal silk back from their larval mouths
and spin a dress fit to protect a queen,
layers of tatted lace at the throat
thickly brailled with her unfinished lyrics.
I'll add it to an armoire of lepidopterous dreams
that dissolve in the cool mornings as we rise
(though when night surrenders the meaning of our days,
they shiver awake again, seeking light).

flutter: carnation
petals fluttered pink,
paper-perfect as we
tossed handfuls of dirt
on your *yiayia's* coffin
she loved carnations
because they last the
longest

WE ARE WHAT WILL BECOME OF US

Strip away the structure, tear down walls, windows, chimneys;
sit back and have a soak, feel the tub pick up its feet,
dragging you – with its spout and exposed plumbing –
clear of your moorings, back to the ocean
where we all began and begin again.

    soak: I set aside
    the soybeans
    to soak overnight, and
    forgot   three days later
    their black husks split
    open, yellow pods
    shooting blind white
    tendrils into the air,
    seeking sun

Had you known this thing or two earlier
would your life have been any different?
You know it now, and now seems late,
the days sputtering behind you
like dust against the horizon
or the shimmering after a rainstorm,
pricks of light you could lick from the sky.

You bite down, reclaim life with a well-honed appetite,
muscled from all the training we call growing up.
And moving through it, you befriend gravity
with every weighted step. So perhaps

              now is not too late after all,
just heavier, enriched with grace.

The calamity of age is a long drawn out accident.
Shattering our bodies in painstaking slow motion,
it accrues within us like rust on garden shears:
you don't notice until one day they stop cutting.
With hormonal ferocity the hedge bites back
but it too will see frost in the paned window one day,
press its nose against the shrouded glass. You knock
within these four walls like a spinning top
losing its spin. What's left? The bare nub
of wood and string, your face, your skin.
With no song of beauty to sing your praises
you knuckle under to the confounding math of aging.
Every new year subtracts one more thing –
the names of friends, your driver's license,
certifications, phone numbers, recipes, your keys,
your well-raised kids, the bulbs you planted in the yard,
early-late-mid-spring-summer-autumn perennials
now blooming with perfect orchestration
in your absence.

                Ah yes,
that's what's left – cumulative resonance
of all your songs and subtonal voicings,
the calm assurance of taking on what your hands
can hold – not a whit more – and they hold
very little, less with each passing day.

aging: *when did you get old?* asks my 4-year-old
we're all getting older, even you, I say
so I will be old too?
yes
and when will you be a little girl again?

Dawn unfurls petals from the last cut bud –
undoing not as capitulation, but as choreography,
growth unwinding itself slyly into decline.

And so a precipice darkens the horizon,
but never quite approaches. Instead a plateau
rises to your feet, offering miles more sure footing
than you'd bargained for. You stop second-guessing,
and relax, let your child sleep in,
snap your laptop screen down.

The relinquishing of all you'd fiercely taken up –
it doesn't fall away when you let go, it loosens,
flips to the B side, inscribes the insides of your eyelids
with a new lexicon for dreams: a garter snake
winds round a tree and spits out a red apple,
a cut flower reconceives its vasculation,
while in the dark kitchen the tea kettle settles,
water runs up a cup's side and falls in to full.

Twinning desire and self – in a word it's twocanny,
the closest thing to childhood where
ego is cheek to cheek with its love object.
This is going the wrong way, what I meant to say
is tongue clicks and teeth clasp words anew –
rolling and bursting like cranberries, sour fresh. Life
as you're in it is eye-popping, a fetus kicking
the skin porous between you and all

                that is not you. Listen,
cut magnolias are releasing their fragrance,
ebullience in their moment of death.

death: my child runs to me, throws her chubby arms around my neck   I close my eyes and hug her tight wanting my brother to feel this

Like a Russian doll enrobed within layers of her own skin
I am embedded in a home filled with smells of my cooking,
children who pick up the worst of my mannerisms,
updated versions of myself saying the same thing,
each iteration another wave in the ocean.

Nesting is the body pursuing accretion.
Amassing twig upon twig, the encumbrance
of things is an unwieldy enterprise,
impossible to dismantle without smashing.

So we get lost hunkering in,
moulding everything to our liking,
butting against one another in our
walled palace of deep sleep.

Sliding cold feet into slippers, I stand
on this magnetic point of earth where
all my filings cohere and become
the bedrock from whence my story springs.

Half limping I tripped
into a night of damp needles,
death and earth underfoot
even as new needles
bristle through skins of bark.
We prickle into being
with throatfuls of hope
arpeggiating with
always more
pushing for
never getting enough
air to voice this
spring run-off.
Water-logged,
the slag heap
leaches phosphorus
into the fields,
fertilizing. In spite of
our reservations
we tumble into
what will become of us.

heap: sitting in her wheelchair mom skinned the late peaches, their slick, orange flesh glistening as they tumbled into the plastic tub   she used them all, no matter how blemished saying, *bruises bring more flavour*

Something in the song that's been playing in my head is reminiscent
of the crazed spinning of my younger days when all the pieces
didn't fit. Mind and heart courting each other from afar,
come together now, the years settle like formed-to-fit pieces,
culled and reshaped for my body, and here I am wearing
the plummiest frock for tomorrow's party – hell, why wait
for tomorrow, the party is now and this dress, this room,
the entire world is spinning, and I am finding centre.

heart: to you my
simplest of kisses for
once and again you
bring me to a place
where all weapons
drop   the stilled
heart proliferates,
entering the senses,
until every fingertip,
tongue, taste bud and
hair follicle chants the
same song

ACKNOWLEDGEMENTS

Some of the poems in this book were previously published in *The Literary Review of Canada*, *This Magazine*, *The IV Lounge Reader* (Insomniac Press), *Drunken Boat*, *Alphabet City: Food Edition*, and *Body Language: A Head to Toe Anthology* (Black Moss Press). A suite of poems were also broadcast on CBC Radio One.

I'd like to acknowledge the generous assistance of the Ontario Arts Council.

I'd also like to thank Alayna Munce, a beautiful writer and a tirelessly committed editor whose generosity of mind made this book what it is today. She read several versions of this manuscript, culled the best work from the lot, and helped me reshape and refine the work. Thank you Alayna. Thank you also to Maureen Scott Harris whose poetic eye helped me improve poems even as we entered the final stages of copy-edit. I have friends and colleagues who have read all or parts of this manuscript at different stages and given me encouragement and advice: Karen Connelly, Diana Fitzgerald Bryden, Anar Ali, Noelle Allen, Priscilla Uppal, Chris Doda, Natalee Caple, Paul Vermeersch, Andrea Cohen. Thank you.

This book is about family and aging, among other things, and I am lucky to be surrounded by a loving family. Thank you Neil, Zara, and Aster, you are the marrow in my bones. You are so much a part of me, I cannot begin to put into words how much I love you. Thank you to my mom, dad and brother Barry, and to all my extended family who have been supportive and inspiring in different ways: the Kim family, the Lee family, and the Shin clan, particularly Sook-ja and the cousins I grew up with in Vancouver and Toronto. Thank you Deedee, Donny, Shirley, Mickey, the Moscoe family, and the Ginsberg family.

There is a constellation of other people I need to thank who have touched me deeply and so inform this poetry. Victoria my abiding friend, thank you. Thank you Costa for allowing me to share some of your family in these poems. Thank you Dennis. Thank you Richard. Thank you Mary Ann. Cousin Frank I am thinking of you and wish you well, as we all do.

This is also in memory of dear family who are not with us anymore:

>   my brother Chris
>   Neil's sister Karen
>   Uncle Jin-soo
>   Auntie Young-soon
>   my dear, dear grandmother.

They have each affected me and my family deeply, and our lives are still humming with the reverberations of their passing.

Raised on a farm in BC's Fraser Valley, *Ann Shin* now lives in Toronto with her husband and two daughters. An award-winning filmmaker and new media producer, she recently directed and produced the documentary *Defector: Escape from North Korea*. Ann's first book of poetry, *The Last Thing Standing,* was published by Mansfield Press in 2002. She is currently at work on a novel.